THE
CONTROL OF
INFLATION

BY

J. E. MEADE

Professor of Political Economy in the
University of Cambridge

AN INAUGURAL LECTURE
DELIVERED IN CAMBRIDGE
ON 4 MARCH 1958

T0346115

CAMBRIDGE
AT THE UNIVERSITY PRESS
1958

CAMBRIDGE UNIVERSITY PRESS
Cambridge, New York, Melbourne, Madrid, Cape Town,
Singapore, São Paulo, Delhi, Tokyo, Mexico City

Cambridge University Press
The Edinburgh Building, Cambridge CB2 8RU, UK

Published in the United States of America by
Cambridge University Press, New York

www.cambridge.org
Information on this title: www.cambridge.org/9781107646803

© Cambridge University Press 1958

First published 1958
First paperback edition 2011

A catalogue record for this publication is available from the British Library

ISBN 978-1-107-64680-3 Paperback

THE CONTROL OF INFLATION

I

THE purpose of this lecture is to consider how one can best put a stop to the inflation of prices. But before we try to find the answer it is useful to know whether this is an important question or not. For the extent to which we should be prepared to recast our present policies and institutions in order to avoid an inflation of prices will depend upon the importance which we attach to the objective of stable prices.

If it were a question of stopping a serious price deflation, it would be a waste of time to ask whether the objective was an important one. Such a deflationary fall in selling prices, when money wage rates cannot easily be lowered, will impede economic growth and raise unemployment. This has been a familiar and agreed theme among economists since the Great Depression of the 1930's. But during the last decade prices in this country have been rising by 4 or 5 per cent per annum, and it is worth pausing to ask whether we need to make any very great efforts to prevent a continuing inflation of money prices and costs of this kind. Might we not remain content with policies and institutions which were such as to avoid deflations, even if they resulted in some such degree of continuing price inflation?

Indeed, a moderate and steady rate of price inflation may have some beneficial effects. It may relieve the community from the dead hand of debt. A large national debt, in my opinion, introduces more serious deadening disincentives into the economy than are generally realised. Between 1948 and 1957 the general level of prices rose by some 50 per cent, which is sufficient to reduce by one-third the real value of a given money debt. We did not remove our great war debt by a levy or repudiation; but its weight has been substantially reduced through inflation.

But is this an equitable way of dealing with the problem? The first main argument against inflation is that it causes an inequitable redistribution between property fixed in terms of money and other forms of property and between incomes fixed in terms of money and other incomes. The old-age pensioner and the parents drawing family allowances have received less than was planned for them; and in such cases it is not the rich who have been soaked. Nor is there any reason to believe that it is the millionaire who keeps his property in the form of Consols and life insurance policies, and the widows and orphans who hold ordinary shares. Indeed, the contrary is much more nearly true. It would at least be a much more rational method of redistribution to keep the value of money constant and then consciously to control by other means the real income and wealth of pensioners, parents, widows, and orphans.

It may be argued that an easier, and to that extent more desirable, way of dealing with this aspect of inflation is to take measures to insure the recipients of fixed or sluggish incomes against the evils of price inflation rather than to put a stop to the inflation itself. Thus money wage rates can be tied to a cost-of-living index. Similarly, proposals have recently been made to tie the money value of old-age pensions or of other social security benefits to the cost-of-living or to an index of the rise of other money incomes in the economy; and such arrangements would guarantee the recipients of such incomes against future inflations. I do not wish to argue against these proposals. On grounds of social justice it is right and proper that we should decide what real share in the national income we want such people to receive. But I do wish to stress that such measures must not be regarded as making the control of inflation less necessary. Indeed, in certain important respects their institution would make such control even more necessary.

There are certain ways in which the tying of previously fixed or sluggish incomes to a price index would increase the dangers of inflation.

Fundamentally, an inflationary pressure is generated when the slices which various independent competing groups of citizens attempt to take out of the national cake together add up to more than the whole cake. Various groups of workers and producers press up their money wages or profit margins by, say, 8 per cent; since some citizens have incomes fixed in terms of money, this 8 per cent rise in variable wages and profits represents, say, a 6 per cent increase in total money incomes; but only, say, 2 per cent more is being produced; 6 per cent more money incomes chase only 2 per cent more goods, and prices are driven up; and in consequence part of the combined claims of producers with variable incomes for an 8 per cent increase in their real incomes is frustrated by a rise in prices and the cost-of-living. Now the more rapidly and completely their claims for increased real rewards are frustrated by a rise in the cost-of-living, the sooner are these groups likely to repeat their claims for yet another substantial increase in money rewards. The larger is the other class of citizens whose incomes are fixed or sluggish in terms of money, the less complete or immediate will be the frustration of those who are pushing up their money rewards. The latter can make real gains at the expense of the former. But the experience of inflation may cause more and more wage rates, as well as such incomes as pensions, to be tied *de facto* or *de jure* to the cost-of-living; and in so far as those who previously had fixed or sluggish money incomes now join in the game and have their money incomes raised quickly in response to price rises, they will accelerate the increase in expenditure on the limited real output of the community. The inflationary process will be speeded up and wage demands will follow one upon another so much the more rapidly.

We all have a certain money illusion. We think of our income in terms of money and we have ideas in our head as to what is the proper sort of money price to pay for this or that service or product. A reasonably effi-

8

cient monetary system for financing transactions and for recording commercial values is of inestimable importance in any modern society. The existence of such a system rests in considerable measure upon our continuing to think in terms of money. Measures like the tying of money wage rates or of old-age pensions to a cost-of-living are an invitation to abandon this most desirable habit of mind. The more people concentrate their thoughts not on their money incomes but on their real incomes, the more rapidly will they try to get rid of their money when they expect prices to rise; and this attempt to fly from money into goods will itself increase money expenditure upon goods and will force prices up so much the higher and the more rapidly. The ultimate end is a complete distrust of the currency and the disorganisation of business which ensues when there is no readily acceptable counter for transactions; but some inefficiencies will be introduced into the economic system before this ultimate disintegration is at all nearly reached.

There remains a final, and for a country like the United Kingdom probably a decisive, reason why it is desirable to attempt to control inflation. The United Kingdom has very important trade relations with the outside world. Moreover, her financial relations with outside countries are close and important; indeed, she acts as the banker for a number of other important countries. If money incomes, prices, and costs are inflated in the United Kingdom more rapidly than in other countries, then citizens in the United Kingdom will tend to increase their purchases of imports and they will find difficulty in selling their high-cost produce in foreign markets. We shall lose reserves of gold and dollars. There will be a recurrence of the only too familiar balance-of-payments crisis. The means of dealing with this are limited. Imports might be restricted by import licensing; but if our prices and costs are continually getting more and more out of line with those of our competitors, the strain on our balance of payments will become greater and greater, and the import restrictions will have to become more and more severe. This would be a very serious development for a country like the United Kingdom which has to import so much of its essential raw materials and foodstuffs. Or we could devalue the pound in an attempt to bring down our prices and costs in terms of foreign currencies. But if speculators expected the domestic inflation to continue in the United Kingdom at a rate more rapid than in other countries, they would expect a series of such devaluations to be necessary. They would attempt to anticipate this by getting out of sterling into other currencies; this would cause a heavy loss of gold and dollar reserves or, if it were allowed to affect the rate of exchange, it would drive the foreign exchange value of the pound still lower and would raise the price in terms of sterling of all imports whose prices were fixed in terms of foreign currencies; this by raising the cost-of-living at home might give rise to still greater demands for increases in money rewards and so extend still further the vicious spiral of higher prices leading to higher wages leading to higher costs leading to higher prices. In the case of a country which, like the United

Kingdom, acts as banker for many persons and institutions in the rest of the world, it is especially important to avoid such a distrust of the national currency.

II

I personally find little difficulty in reaching the conclusion that inflation as well as deflation is an evil which deserves a very real effort to avoid. But let us be very clear that there are worse evils than inflation. The stagnation of the 1930's is a much worse evil than the inflation of the 1950's. We must give very careful thought to the question whether a serious attempt to prevent a continuation of the inflation of money prices would lead to a cessation of growth of economic output and to a rise in the general level of unemployment. It is worth a real effort to stop inflation but it must not be done by methods which prevent high and rising production.

In order to decide whether, and, if so, how, price inflation can be stopped without endangering employment and production it is necessary to consider the mechanism through which price rises are generated. There are two closely interrelated factors at work, one operating through the level of money demand for goods and services and the other through the level of money costs of the factors of production and, in particular, through the level of money wage rates. Let us first analyse each of these two factors separately, and then consider the relationship between them.

Suppose first that all money wage rates are fixed. Something then causes an increase in the level of total money expenditure on goods and services. When the demand for their finished products goes up producers can do either of two things; they can produce and sell more at an unchanged price or they can raise the price at which they sell an unchanged output. In fact they are likely to react partly in the one manner and partly in the other. If there is much unemployed labour and unused productive capacity, then an increase in demand is likely to lead to a large increase in output and little rise in price. But as demand increases to higher levels, there are likely to arise bottlenecks in one industry after another, as reserves of suitable unemployed labour disappear and productive capacity is strained, until in the end it is impossible to produce more in any industry so that an increase in money expenditure on goods and services will cause only a rise in their prices. In more technical language, with a constant money wage rate the short-run elasticity of supply of goods in general is likely to be nearly infinite when there is mass unemployment but to fall towards zero as the point of full employment is reached. Thus with constant money wage rates prices are likely to be at a lower level when demand is low and at a higher level when demand is high. But this does not, of course, explain why prices should continue to rise as they have done over the last decade at a rate of 4 or 5 per cent per annum.

To explain this, we must turn to the other side of the picture. Money wage rates are not in fact constant and in the last decade they have been rising more quickly than productivity with the result that money costs per unit of output have been rising. In the jargon of economists the supply-curve itself has been rising through time. In recent years money earnings per head have been rising by about 7 per cent per annum and output per head by a little over 2 per cent per annum. In consequence labour costs per unit of output have been rising by more than 4 per cent per annum. The steady rise of prices over the last decade is certainly very intimately connected with this steady rise of money costs of production.

But why do rates of money earnings rise more quickly than productivity? In order to answer this question it is necessary to consider the relationship between the demand influences and the cost influences. When the level of demand is high three influences are brought to work which are likely to make wage rates rise at a rapid rate. First, the high level of demand for finished products will give rise to a high level of demand for labour by producers; the volume of unemployment will be low and the number of unfilled vacancies will be high; and wage-earners will be in a strong position to bargain for increases in rates of pay. Secondly, a high level of demand for finished products will, as we have seen, cause the prices of finished products to be high relatively to any given level of money wage rates; when prices and the cost-of-living are high relatively to money wage rates, workers will have an added reason to demand higher rates of pay to restore the real purchasing power of their wages. Thirdly, when demand rises profits will be raised, either because a larger output is produced at any given margin of profit or else because prices are raised relatively to wage rates so that a higher profit margin is obtained on any given output; in either case higher profits mean that each employer can afford more easily to pay higher rates of wages and the resistance of employers to wage claims will be lower. In brief, a high level of demand is likely to raise prices relatively to any given level of money wage rates; but also by reducing unemployment, increasing the number of unfilled vacancies, raising the cost-of-living, and raising the profitability of industry it is likely to set the conditions in which wages will rise more rapidly than productivity so that there is a continuing inflation of the whole structure of money prices, money costs, and money incomes.

With this brief description of the process of price inflation we are now in a position to consider the measures which might be taken to avoid it. The authorities have at their disposal certain instruments of control through which they can influence the general level of demand for goods and services. They can themselves reduce government expenditure; they can raise rates of taxation so that private citizens are left with smaller tax-free incomes to spend; or by a tighter monetary policy they can make it more difficult for businessmen to raise funds for capital development. If our analysis is correct such a reduction in total monetary demand will cause some fall in selling prices relatively to money wage rates and other costs, as producers find the markets for their products becoming less easy. Producers will, however, also react by producing less and employing less labour. In the ways already indicated, the fall in prices, profit margins, and employment will all combine to alter the atmosphere in the labour market, so that money wage rates rise less rapidly. There is presumably some point at which the total demand for products has been so reduced that the conditions in the labour market have been so eased that money wage rates rise at a rate equal to the rate of rise in productivity, so that wage costs per unit of output remain constant. This we may call the 'break-even' point.

Thus price inflation *can* be prevented by a sufficiently severe policy of restraint in monetary and budgetary policies; but an essential part of this mechanism is a restriction of total demand which will, *inter alia*, so raise the level of unemployment relatively to the level of unfilled vacancies that the break-even point is reached at which money wage rates cease to rise more rapidly than productivity. Price stability may be compatible with 3 per cent but not with only 1 per cent of workers unemployed.

We can put the problem in its most dramatic form by asking what would happen if the authorities desired actually to reduce the general level of prices—a situation which might arise in actual fact if an attempt were made to stabilise the general level of prices and if, for some reason or another, prices had temporarily risen above the level at which they were being stabilised. In this case the authorities by more restrictive monetary and fiscal policies would reduce the level of total money expenditure on goods and services. In so far as producers reacted to this by lowering the prices (and so the profit margins) at which they were willing to sell their existing level of output, this would be the end of the story. But suppose that producers' reaction to a fall in the demand for their products were of exactly the opposite kind; suppose that they added a fixed profit margin to their variable costs (such as their wage bill) and that they simply reduced the amount which they produced at this more or less constant 'full-cost' price. When output had been so reduced that the demand for labour fell below the 'break-even' point, wage rates would rise less quickly than productivity. With fixed profit margins selling prices would come down as labour costs per unit of output fell; and by this process the price level could gradually be brought back to the desired lower level. The pains of price stabilisation can thus be seen to depend upon three factors: (1) the extent to which producers would in fact reduce output and not prices when demand fell, (2) the extent to which wages would continue to rise in spite of a rise in the ratio of unemployed persons to unfilled vacancies, and (3) the speed with which it was desired to bring prices back to the target level if they should diverge temporarily from it.

The nature of the main issues should now be clear. First, should the government take the plunge and say that, whatever happens, it is going to control the level of monetary expenditure so that prices do not permanently rise above a given ceiling? Secondly, if the government does take the plunge, is it possible so to mould the institutional arrangements in the labour market that the 'break-even' point at which wage rates cease to rise more rapidly than productivity is reached at a satisfactorily high level of employment and production? But these two questions presuppose that the government can in fact exercise a continuous and effective control over total monetary demand. Whether or not existing controls over demand are adequate is a third basic issue. It is to these three questions which we must now turn.

III

What is exactly meant by 'taking the plunge'? The government would announce that in future it was going to make full use of its powers of monetary and budgetary policy in order to maintain the total monetary demand for goods and services at the highest possible level which was compatible with the prevention of some stated index of the selling prices of final products from rising above a stated ceiling. As I shall argue in a moment, if it is decided that price inflation must really be stopped, there are great advantages in the government committing itself to the prevention of some precisely defined index of prices from rising above some precisely defined level. But before this case is argued it is necessary to consider for a moment the nature of the price index to which any such commitment should refer.

Suppose that the cost-of-living index were chosen for this purpose. Suppose then that the terms of international trade were to move against this country because the price of imports had risen. A decline in the real incomes of consumers would have occurred for reasons quite out of the control of the United Kingdom authorities. But in order to stabilise the cost-of-living when the import component in the cost-of-living rose, the authorities would have to take disinflationary measures to drive down the price of home-produced goods to offset the rise in the price of imported goods. But unless money wage rates could be quickly reduced *pari passu* with the fall in the prices of domestic products, there might be a serious growth of unemployment.

An exactly similar difficulty would arise if the government were to decide to raise more revenue by way of indirect taxes. The consequent rise in the price charged to consumers of beer, tobacco, or whatever other commodity was taxed, would have to be offset by a deflation in the prices of other products. Once again, unless wages and other money costs could be as promptly reduced, unemployment might result.

For the same reason, it would be wise to exclude from the index such prices as house rents which are still subject to extensive direct controls. Whether, and, if so, to what extent, rents should be decontrolled is a major issue of economic policy affecting the distribution of income and the uses of house property. But if a government does decide that rents should be raised by decontrol, it would be irrational and possibly disastrous economically to combine this with another set of rules which involved deflating total demand until the selling prices of other products had been reduced to offset the rise of decontrolled rents.

The best price index to choose for our purpose would thus appear to be one which was specially constructed to cover the selling prices of all domestically produced goods and services except those subject to price control, excluding from such prices the import content of home production and indirect taxes.[1] But, if some such index is chosen, there are powerful arguments in favour of taking the plunge and guaranteeing that it will not be allowed to rise above a given ceiling.

First, the setting of a precise ceiling to a precise price index would have the advantage of calling powerful forces of private speculation to the aid of the authorities. The relevant price index would be frequently and promptly published; if ever it was above the ceiling level, it would be known that the authorities would take disinflationary steps to bring prices down, and private purchasers would have an incentive to postpone their purchases until prices were no longer above the ceiling level; and when the price level was below the ceiling level, purchasers would be induced to speed up their expenditure in order to come into the market before the expansion of monetary demand by the authorities had raised prices once more to their ceiling level. Such speculative postponements and anticipations of private expenditure would powerfully reinforce the actions of the authorities.

Second, a firm commitment to stabilise domestic prices would transform our balance-of-payments problems. Of course, if domestic financial policy is aimed exclusively at the maintenance of domestic demand at the highest level compatible with a ceiling to a domestic price level, then it cannot at the same time be

[1] But including subsidies. It is the net price received by home producers which we want to stabilise.

used to control the balance of foreign payments. It will no longer be permissible to take disinflationary measures at home simply in order to discourage the purchase of imports and to release home supplies for export, so as to improve the balance of payments and to stop a foreign drain of gold reserves. But those deficits in the balance of payments which arise from an uncontrolled inflationary rise of prices, costs, and buying power within the United Kingdom would automatically cease; and this would be no mean contribution to the preservation of external equilibrium. It is still possible to imagine circumstances in which, for one reason or another beyond our power of control, the foreign demand for United Kingdom produce would fall off even in these conditions. This would lead to a decline in our exports and so to the growth of a deficit on our balance of payments, which we would not be prepared to offset by engineering an actual deflation in the price level of our own domestic output and in the money-incomes of our producers.

The answer to this difficulty is easy to find. The rate of exchange between the pound sterling and foreign currencies should be allowed to vary. If then there were some foreign shift of demand away from our products, the pound would depreciate somewhat; this would cheapen our exports in foreign currencies; and it would raise the price of our imports in sterling. This in due course would so expand our exports and contract our imports as to restore equilibrium to our balance-of-payments. Meanwhile, if the pound threatened to depreciate excessively, speculators—firm in the knowledge that the sterling price of our own domestic output was to be held stable—would purchase sterling and thus support its value until the long-run equilibrating forces of the exchange-rate change had had time to restore our balance of payments.

But this is much too apologetic a way for me to speak of the balance-of-payments aspect of proposals for setting a firm ceiling to domestic prices. If we really could stabilise the sterling price of our own products, then so long as any price inflation was expected to continue in the rest of the world there would be an underlying tendency for the pound to appreciate in the foreign exchange markets. Even if all foreign inflations were brought under control, there would be more or less equal chances of the pound appreciating or depreciating and in any case no chance of any enormous depreciation of the pound. The only chance of a substantial depreciation of the pound would be the possibility of a serious deflation of money incomes and prices in the United States and elsewhere. But the 1930's have shown that in such circumstances, in order to avoid deflationary influences, overseas countries are likely to hitch their currencies to the pound rather than to the dollar. Indeed, I would go so far as to argue that the only way in which we can hope to continue to combine the role of international banker with our present very exiguous reserves of foreign exchange is to give the foreigner a firm confidence in the stability of the real purchasing power of our currency rather than in the fixity of its price in terms of other currencies. In such circumstances I would expect it to fare very well.

A third important argument in favour of the setting of a ceiling to a precise price index of selling prices is that it would indirectly help in restraining the inflationary rise of money costs. If there were real confidence that the general level of selling prices would not be inflated, there would be a double restraining influence on wage-rate adjustments. Employers in general would not expect to be able easily to offset increased labour costs by raising selling prices; they would be more resistant to wage demands. On the other hand, the workers would not expect rises in the cost of living arising from domestic inflationary tendencies; and in so far as the expectation of future rises in prices influences their wage demands they would show more restraint. Moreover, the trade unions would realise that too rapid a rise in wage costs might lead now to a redundancy of labour, since it could no longer be offset by a rise of selling prices.

IV

There are, therefore, some very powerful arguments in favour of the government committing itself to a precise ceiling for selling prices. But can we be certain that there would remain no problem on the side of costs? It depends upon how ambitious we are in defining the level of full employment which we hope to attain. As we have already argued, other things being equal, the lower the number of unemployed workers and the higher the number of unfilled vacancies, the more rapidly are wage rates likely to rise. To repeat our previous example, in conditions of price stability wage rates might not rise more rapidly than productivity if the unemployment percentage were 3, but nevertheless might do so if the demand for labour were so high that only 1 per cent were unemployed.

But can anything be done to shift the 'break-even' point in the labour market at which wage rates rise only as quickly as productivity?

It is important to realise that nothing important can be done on the lines of tying wage rates in particular industries and occupations to changes in productivity in those same industries and occupations. An example will demonstrate this point. Suppose that there are only two products, agricultural output and industrial output. Suppose further that technical progress is such that in the course of the year productivity does not rise in manufactures but rises by 5 per cent in agriculture. If wage rates remained unchanged, the cost and price of agricultural produce might fall by a full 5 per cent. But the stabilisation of the general level of prices would involve the stimulation of total demand until the general level of prices had been raised back to its old level. This might mean that the price of manufactures had to be raised 2½ per cent above the initial level while the price of agricultural produce was pulled half way back to its initial level, so that it fell by only 2½ instead of 5 per cent. The competition for labour between the two industries might then lead to a bidding up of the wage rate by 2½ per cent in both industries. In this case the industrial workers would enjoy a rise of wage rates by 2½ per cent even though their productivity had not increased, and the agricultural workers would enjoy a rise of wage rates by only $2\frac{1}{2}$ per cent even though their productivity had risen by 5 per cent.

Indeed, the outcome for some time might well have to be even more favourable to the industrial workers whose productivity had not increased. Suppose that when people's real incomes rise (as they would when productivity in agriculture rose) consumers want to buy little more agricultural products but many more industrial products. Then labour will become redundant in agriculture where output per head has gone up but the demand for the product has scarcely risen, and labour will be scarce in industry where output per head has not risen but the demand for the product has increased. There will be a tendency for prices to fall further in agriculture where there is now a glut of produce and to rise further in industry where there is a shortage of produce. This should be allowed to lead to a rise in industrial wage rates relatively to agricultural wage rates so long as it is necessary to attract workers from agriculture to industry. The rise in productivity is in agriculture but the consequential rise in wages should be in industry.

When against a background of a stable general average of prices for finished products, there are a series of increases of productivity at varying rates in different industries and occupations, redundancy of labour may appear in some industries, occupations, and regions, and shortages of labour in other industries, occupations, and regions; and there will be no obvious simple connection between the rate of increase of productivity in any one industry, occupation, or region, and the redundancy or shortage of labour in that industry, occupation, or region. Wage rates must rise in those parts of the economy in which these developments tend to cause a shortage of labour relatively to wage rates in those parts of the economy in which these developments tend to cause a redundancy of labour. Any attempt to preserve pre-existing differentials by raising wage rates in the latter group of industries to catch up those in the former group can only lead to a general upward pressure on wage costs which will adversely affect the 'break-even' point in the labour market.

Closely connected with this is another negative conclusion about wage-fixing arrangements. The fixing of money wage rates must not be regarded as the ultimate weapon for affecting the general distribution of the national income between wage-earners on the one hand and other classes in the community on the other hand. Money wage rates in general can be pushed up to a certain level at the expense of profits; but in a market in which a ceiling has been set to the prices at which the products of labour can be sold, a rise in wage rates beyond this point will cause unemployment. Any further redistribution must be sought through other means. For example, measures to prevent monopolies and so to increase competition between producers are likely to raise the demand for labour and so to raise the general level of money wage rates which is at any time compatible with a constant level of selling prices; the type of taxes which are imposed and, in its broadest sense, the social security system which is in operation will greatly affect the distribution of incomes between various classes of citizen; and as a longer term consideration, changes might be made in death duties, in the laws of inheritance, and in certain other institutions in order to bring about a more equal distribution in the ownership of property and in the enjoyment of profits themselves. The ultimate redistribution of income and wealth between individual citizens must be sought by means of this kind and not through wage policy.

But are there any positive improvements which can be made in our present wage-fixing arrangements which might favourably affect the 'break-even' point? I shall not consider such revolutionary changes as that employers' associations and trade unions be made illegal as monopolies in restraint of trade, or that the government itself should fix wage rates in a comprehensive national wages policy. Present procedures of wage negotiation will certainly continue. But within this framework there are some possible improvements to be made.

The atmosphere of wage negotiations might be much influenced if somebody—perhaps a permanent form of the present Council on Prices, Productivity and Incomes—were required to make regular estimates of the percentage increase in the general level of money wage rates which would be compatible in the coming year with the preservation of full employment in a regime of stable selling prices. Crystal-gazing about future economic trends is not a thing which I generally recommend. But in this case it is a matter of saying that wage rates should go up by something like 2 to 3 per cent per annum (which is the order of magnitude of the annual rate of increase in productivity) instead of by something like 7 per cent per annum (as they have done in recent years). The Council should, of course, make the best estimate that it can. But if this year it says 2 per cent when it should have said 3 per cent or vice versa, no irreparable damage will have been done. If wages have gone up this year a little less quickly than they should, then they should go up next year a little more quickly than would otherwise have been appropriate. And the need for this will become apparent, because too slow a rise in money wage rates will, at constant selling prices, lead to a growing scarcity of labour and vice versa.

But, as we have already seen, it is necessary not only that the general level of money wage rates should not go up more quickly than productivity. It is also necessary that wage rates should go up rather more quickly than the average in those industries, occupations, and regions where a local scarcity of labour is developing, and rather less quickly than the average where local redundancies of labour are developing. In fact there is likely to be a strong tendency for the rate of increase of money wage rates which the Council on Prices, Productivity and Incomes ruled to be possible on the average for industry as a whole to be treated by the workers in each particular industry as the minimum rise to which they are themselves entitled. If this were so, the announcement of a suitable average wage increase might do more harm than good. This danger would be lessened and the necessary adjustment of relative wage rates would be helped if a new arbitral body or set of arbitral bodies were instituted for the sole purpose of giving an opinion whether in any particular case a rate of rise of wages appreciably above or below the average was necessary in order, over the next few years, to avoid a serious local shortage or redundancy of labour. If it could be accepted as an obligation by the main parties to wage negotiations always, at the request of either of the negotiating parties or of the government, to refer to this arbitral body for an opinion on this question of fact, the final outcome of negotiations might well be influenced in a salutary manner.

The 'break-even' point in the labour market will also be greatly affected by the degree of mobility of the labour force. Suppose that at any one time it is proposed to reduce the level of unemployment from 500,000 to 300,000 workers. Consider two alternative methods of achieving this objective. The 500,000 unemployed workers will be attached to certain industries, occupations, and regions; and at the same time there will be some unfilled vacancies in some other industries, occupations and regions. If it were possible for the unemployed workers to move readily to the unfilled vacancies, unemployment could be reduced without any very substantial change in the upward pressure on wage rates in the economy as a whole. For while the bargaining power of labour would be somewhat increased in those parts of the economy from which the labour was moving, it would be somewhat decreased in those parts of the economy into which labour was moving. Contrast this with a policy of reducing the level of unemployment from 500,000 to 300,000 by a general expansion of the money demand for goods and services without any significant mobility of labour. The demand for labour would have to be raised in all industries, occupations, and regions (both in those in which there was a redundancy and also in those in which there was already a shortage of labour) until the market for labour had been expanded by the required 200,000 in the industries, occupations, and regions to which the unemployed were already attached. There would be a great increase in the upward pressure on wage rates throughout the economy. Thus the 'break-even' point in the labour market can be achieved with a lower level of unemployment, the more mobile is the labour force.

For this reason, if it is desired to combine full employment with price stability, it would be well worth-while applying greater thought and expenditure of resources to such problems as the retraining, removal, and rehousing of unemployed workers and their families.

Moreover, there are a number of practices in the labour market which reduce the mobility and flexibility of the labour force. Demarcation rules which prevent one body of workers from shifting from one job to another, apprenticeship rules which prevent the easy entry of new labour into expanding trades, and insistence upon national bargaining which makes it difficult to adapt the conditions of work to the needs of particular producers, are important examples. The more effectively such practices can be restrained, the easier it will be to combine full employment with price stability.

V

We must turn now to the question whether the government in fact has at its disposal adequate instruments of control over the general level of monetary demand for goods and services. We must consider not only whether the authorities can raise or lower expenditures by a sufficient amount but also whether they can make such adjustments sufficiently promptly. For speed is at least as important as size of response.

Inflations and deflations of demand largely feed upon themselves. If prices and profits start on an upward movement, this may well lead to an anticipation of a still further rise; and this speculative optimism may well cause a further increase in demand which will itself drive prices and profits up still more. If it had been possible by a prompt mechanism of control to nip the incipient inflation of demand in the bud, then the inflationary pressures might never have gathered force. An early control of an inflation of demand is likely to require considerably less powerful intervention than a delayed control.

There is an even more serious possibility if action is delayed. Suppose that (for reasons which we shall examine later) there is still a considerable time-lag between any inflationary or deflationary change in the economic climate and the taking of counter-measures by the authorities. It is possible that in these conditions the counter-measures will make the situation worse instead of improving it. Consider a sequence of un-controlled inflationary pressure which would rise to a peak and then of itself turn down into some deflationary fall in prices, profits, output and employment; we may think of one of the periods of inflationary pressure followed by minor recessions which have occurred in the United States economy since the end of the Second World War. Suppose that the authorities wish to offset this movement; they impose more and more stringent disinflationary measures as the inflationary pressure in the economy becomes more and more intense; but there are delays which mean that the authorities' dis-inflationary measures are in fact geared to the degree of inflationary pressure to be offset some period—say six months—previously. Consider the effect of this policy at the time when the inflationary boom ends and turns down into a recession. Six months after the top of the boom, when uncontrolled deflationary forces have had six months to gather momentum, the controlled dis-inflationary forces exerted by the counter-inflationary measures of the authorities will be at their maximum. This might be sufficient to send the economic system into a nose dive of deflation. And conversely, in any situation in which the economic system is naturally moving from the bottom of a recession into a period of economic expansion, the fact that the authorities' re-flationary measures will be at their maximum six months after the bottom of the depression, when re-covery has had that much time to gather force, might set in motion speculative forces of expansion which would turn a moderate and useful recovery into an undesirable inflation. It is at least possible that delayed counter-measures would make fluctuations greater than they would have been in the absence of all counter-measures. In the words of the poet, delayed action might accentuate the tendency for us to

>...swerve
>Along our sinusoidal curve.

Some delay between any undesired disturbance and the corrective action is inevitable. First, there will be a delay between the occurrence of the initial change and its realisation by the authorities. Secondly, there will be some constitutional, administrative, and political causes for delay between the realisation of the initial change and the taking of counter-measures by the authorities. Thirdly, there will be some delay between the taking of the counter-measures by the authorities and the full development of the actual effects of these counter-measures upon the economic situation.

The first of these three delays is common to all forms of control, and I shall not give much thought to it to-day. But for the response by the authorities to be as prompt as possible much effort should be put into the full and prompt statistical reporting of changes in the main relevant economic variables—prices, employment, unemployment, output, sales, stocks, imports, exports, etc.[1]

[1] Such prompt reporting of actual changes may, of course, be usefully supplemented by information (such as information on producers' plans for future expenditures on capital development)

As far as the delay between the realisation of the need for action and the actual change of policy is concerned, monetary policy could score high marks. A small and desirable change in conventional procedures would enable the Bank of England to raise or lower the Bank Rate on any working day in the year, and it can already purchase or sell long-term securities in the market in any amounts at any time in order to pump funds into or out of the capital market. Moreover, such open-market operations need not be publicised; they can be made as soon as the need for action seems probable; and the Bank should not be inhibited as the situation develops from reversing next week or next month some open-market purchase or sale which it has undertaken today.

But in so far as the lag between a change in policy and its actual effect upon the economy is concerned, monetary policy probably scores badly. Any effect which a rise in the short-term rate of interest may have upon the holding of stocks may be reasonably prompt in its effect; but this is not likely to be the main ultimate effect of a change in monetary policy, and the other ultimate effects are all likely to be delayed. When the Bank of England takes steps to reduce the liquidity of the commercial banks, the latter may be induced to reduce their advances to industry. But with the British overdraft system this process is likely to be delayed. The process must consist of being less willing to grant new over-

which may help to forecast movements likely to take place in some of the variables after the date for which the last actual values are known.

33

draft facilities, of increasing pressure on clients to repay their outstanding borrowings from the banks concerned, and of negotiating reductions in the limits of unused overdraft facilities. But these things all take time, and if there is a natural inflationary pressure in the economy, business men are likely to continue for a time to make increased use of unused overdraft facilities, so that total advances may well continue to grow for some time after the change in monetary policy. The change in monetary policy may well involve an almost immediate sale of long-term securities by the banks and so an almost immediate rise in long-term interest rates. But any effects which this may have upon expenditure upon capital development are likely to be delayed, since dearer money is likely to affect projects which are now being planned for future execution rather than projects on which funds are now being spent.

As far as budgetary policy is concerned, changes in public expenditure score badly from the point of view of both the types of delay now under discussion. Changes in rates of expenditure on public services require considerable reconsideration of the various public policies involved and are likely to make a considerable political fuss. Moreover, even when a decision has finally been taken to change the level of some government expenditure the consequential change in that level is likely to mature only gradually as the new plan replaces the old.

Changes in rates of taxation are likely to score badly where monetary policy scores well and to score well where monetary policy scores badly. As the tax system is at present organised, there are serious delays between the realisation of a change in the economic situation and the offsetting change in rates of taxation. There are parliamentary and constitutional difficulties in changing rates of tax except at budget time; and there are real administrative difficulties in making frequent changes in many tax rates. Thus with present P.A.Y.E. procedures a change in rates of income-tax requires the preparation and distribution to all employers of new tax-deduction schedules; or a change in the rates of purchase-tax leads to awkward problems of profit or loss on stocks in retailers' hands of goods which have paid tax at the old rates. In any case, a change in tax is a matter of considerable political concern, so that politicians will often have strong incentives to make no change until the need for change has become extreme.

But changes in many taxes are likely to win high marks in so far as the lag between the application of the new rates and the realisation of its effects on expenditure is concerned. For example, a change in the rate of tax collected under P.A.Y.E. will immediately affect the weekly pay packet of millions of wage-earners; or a change in the rate of purchase-tax will very promptly affect the price which all consumers have to pay for the goods in question. It is, of course, probable that some part of the impact effect of such changes may fall upon the savings of wage-earners and other consumers, in which case to this extent there will be no immediate effect upon the amounts of goods which they try to purchase. But the change is likely to affect real expenditure fairly quickly.

In short, a widespread tax would constitute an ideal instrument of control if only it were technically capable of rapid and frequent change and if an institutional arrangement could be found to make such changes politically possible.

VI

In an Annex to the White Paper on Employment Policy issued by the Coalition Government in 1944 (Cmd. 6527) the proposal was made that the workers' and employers' weekly contributions to national insurance might be varied in order to stabilise the general level of money demand for goods and services.[1] Technically, this is among the best forms of levy which could be used for our purpose. It would be possible to make administrative arrangements for prompt and, if necessary, frequent variations in the amount of the levy.

The effect on demand would be marked and prompt in so far as the contributions of the employee or of the self-employed were varied, since this would immediately affect the amount of spendable incomes. A change in the employers' contribution would affect the profitability of business and thus would ultimately affect expenditure out of profits; but such an effect would be uncertain in amount and delayed in its operation. Moreover, a rise in the employers' contributions would raise costs of production; and it would be anomalous to attempt to restrain a rise in money prices

[1] In fact under the post-war legislation reforming the national insurance system the Treasury is already endowed with the power to vary national insurance contributions for this purpose.

by an instrument which directly raised money costs. It would be preferable, though not absolutely essential, that the scheme should exclude variations in employers' contributions.

But could a device of this kind be operated on a scale which was sufficient for the stabilisation of demand? At present national insurance contributions are levied at a fixed rate regardless of the earnings of the contributor in question. For this reason it may be difficult to raise the rate of contribution very significantly because an increased contribution which could fairly easily be borne by a well-paid worker might represent a very heavy burden to a low-paid worker. This difficulty would be diminished if the levy in question were expressed as a proportion of the contributor's actual earnings, as has been proposed in some recent suggestions for the reform of our national insurance arrangements. An additional payment of 1 per cent of the earnings of those concerned would raise something like £150 million a year; and the device could thus be used to exert a really important influence over total demand.

From the point of view of fairness of tax burden an even more acceptable alternative might be a scheme whereby the rate of income-tax was subject to a positive (or negative) supplement which could be varied quarterly. Since many workers are exempt from income-tax it could not have so widespread an effect upon the weekly pay packet as a variation in national insurance contributions. Moreover, it would be administratively more difficult. But it might nevertheless prove a feasible alternative. The income-tax allowances for dependents and for earned income, the amounts of income subject to reduced rates of income-tax, and the standard rate and the reduced rates of income-tax would all, as now, be fixed once a year at budget time. But each quarter positive (or negative) supplements to the standard rate and to the reduced rates of tax could be announced. As far as personal incomes were concerned which, like dividends, could be treated only on an annual basis, the amount of tax liability at the end of the year would be so adjusted that the annual rate of tax was equivalent to the average of the four quarterly supplemented rates which had been announced in the course of the year. But weekly, monthly, or quarterly earnings at present subject to P.A.Y.E. deductions of income-tax would be treated for such deductions on a quarterly instead of an annual basis. Each quarter a new period would start for the reckoning of P.A.Y.E. deductions on the present cumulative principle, and new tax deduction schedules would be used if a change had been announced in the quarterly supplements to the rate of tax.[1] At the end of each year tax payments under P.A.Y.E. would be so adjusted as to make the total tax paid on the whole year's income correspond to an annual rate of tax on that income equivalent to the average of the four quarterly supplemented rates announced during the year.

[1] To avoid delay it might be feasible to have alternative tax deduction schedules printed in advance to correspond to various positive and negative supplements to the normal rates of tax.

I do not want on this occasion to argue the detailed merits and difficulties inherent in these particular schemes. My present intention is only to illustrate the point of principle: it would, in my opinion, be both desirable and possible, at some administrative cost and inconvenience, to devise some form of widespread levy on personal incomes which could be used to make frequent and prompt variations in spendable incomes.

It is, of course, necessary to treat stabilisation policy as a co-ordinated whole. A particularly important example of this truth is provided by the intimate relationship which would have to exist between those in charge of monetary and banking policy and those in charge of the special stabilisation levies. If variations in national insurance contributions were the chosen instrument, arrangements would have to be made to separate the book-keeping of the normal insurance contributions from the excess or deficiency of the contribution which was imposed for stabilisation purposes. This could be achieved by instituting a Stabilisation Fund separate from the ordinary National Insurance Fund. In times of inflationary pressure when contributions had been raised above their normal level, the Stabilisation Fund would receive the revenue from these supplementary contributions. In times of deflationary pressure when contributions had been reduced below their normal level, the Stabilisation Fund would pay out to the National Insurance Fund an amount sufficient to make up this shortfall in its revenue. A similar Stabilisation Fund could be set up to receive from, or to pay to, the Exchequer the proceeds of the special supplements on rates of income tax, if that were the chosen instrument. In either case what the Stabilisation Fund did with its balances would most powerfully affect monetary conditions. Suppose, for example, that when it was receiving funds the Stabilisation Fund invested in Treasury Bills or ran up a deposit balance with the Bank of England; and suppose that when it had to pay out funds, it sold Treasury Bills or ran down or overdrew its account with the Bank of England.

The liquid reserves of the commercial banks would in this case be subject to an automatic drain equal to the total of the supplementary stabilisation levies in times of inflationary pressure. If, for example, £150 million per annum were being drawn out of the commercial banks for the payment of additional levies on personal incomes to the Stabilisation Fund, this would cause the liquid reserves of the commercial banks to decline at a rate of £150 million per annum. As the total liquid reserves of the commercial banks (including cash, money at call, and bills) are now about £2000 million, it can be readily seen that this would represent a powerful automatic force leading to a deflationary monetary policy. And conversely, in times when a counter-measure was required to offset deflationary pressures in the economy, the special reductions in levies on personal incomes would introduce automatically both an increase in the flow of money receipts to consumers to stimulate demand and also an increase in the liquidity of the banking system to enable the banks to adopt a reflationary monetary policy.

Variations in special stabilisation levies could thus be

so operated as to enforce a powerful and continuing monetary disinflation so long as they were kept above the normal, and vice versa when they were reduced below the normal. But whether or not it would be desirable to link these monetary effects with the direct effects of variations in special stabilisation levies upon consumers' expenditure would be a matter for consideration in each particular situation. It might be desirable to offset them in whole or in part by means of open-market purchases or sales of long-term securities by the Bank of England or by shifts between long-term securities and short-term assets on the part of the Stabilisation Fund itself.

The extent to which reliance should be put upon the various instruments of control—the supply of money, the structure of the national debt, normal rates of tax, or variations in special stabilisation levies—will depend upon the particular conditions of each case. How far is speed of response important in the particular circumstances of the case? Which instrument will raise or lower demand in a particular sector of the economic system affected by some special temporary disturbance? Does the balance-of-payments situation require controls which will operate very directly on the demand for imports and for domestic products which could be exported?

Another basic consideration is the choice between instruments of control which affect expenditure on capital development and those which affect the demand for consumption goods. In my previous discussion of the 'break-even' point in the labour market I argued

as if the rate of rise of productivity were a given pheno-
menon about which one could do nothing. But this is
not entirely true; and the more quickly output per head
can be made to rise, the more quickly can money wage
rates be raised without leading to any rise of costs per
unit of output. One way in which productivity can be
raised is by maintaining a high rate of investment in
new capital equipment. To fight a current inflation by
measures which cut down on current consumption
rather than on investment will permit a higher future
rate of increase of productivity and will thus alleviate
future inflationary pressures. On the other hand, the
measures necessary to restrain current consumption
may well themselves intensify the immediate pressure
for increased money wage rates in an attempt to
restore their real standard of living on the part of the
wage-earners. Capital development and the consequential rises in productivity are not merely—indeed
not mainly—needed for the purpose of controlling inflation; they are wanted for their own sake in order to
raise real income and standards of living. But they have
an important effect upon the inflationary process; and
in so far as it is possible to choose weapons of control
which will maintain present rates of investment at the
expense of present rates of consumption without there-
by causing an immediate increase in the demand for
higher money wage rates, future inflationary forces will
be reduced.

But although stabilisation policy must, for these
reasons, be treated as a single co-ordinated whole,
there is, nevertheless, reason for making certain broad

distinctions between responsibility for the various weapons of control. The ordinary budget is used primarily to influence the distribution of income and property, to determine the broad choice between investment and consumption over a period of years, and to subsidise particular activities (such as agriculture) at the cost of others (such as industry); in addition it could and should be used generally to exercise a steady disinflationary or reflationary force during a continuing period of inflationary or deflationary pressure; but it is not well contrived to exercise prompt and frequent disinflationary or reflationary influences over total demand, changing the pressure from month to month as the driver of a motor-car continually presses his steering wheel now slightly to the right and now slightly to the left. Such guidance could be exercised in the monetary sphere by the Bank of England and in the fiscal sphere by the proposed system of variations in some special stabilisation levy on personal incomes.

It can be argued that policies of this latter type should be entrusted to bodies which have been given full power of operation of their stabilisation weapons independently of the government. Chancellors of the Exchequer cannot reasonably be expected in all political situations to take prompt but unpopular action to reduce spendable incomes. They may be greatly tempted to wait and see, and thus to let undesirable tendencies develop much too far unchecked. This danger might be met by some self-denying ordinance by the political parties, removing stabilisation policy from the ordinary political machine.

This end might conceivably be achieved by devising an automatic sliding scale for the operation of the stabilisation devices. Thus in the Coalition Government's White Paper of 1944 it was suggested that the rates of national insurance contributions should vary automatically with variations in the percentage of workers unemployed. When the unemployment percentage went up to a stated level, the rate of contribution would automatically be reduced by a stated amount; and vice versa. This suggestion is open to two serious objections.

In the first place, experience since the war has shown that it is practicable to keep the unemployment percentage consistently at a much lower absolute level than was then envisaged. The unemployment percentage is not likely to prove the sensitive and variable index which would be appropriate for the workings of an automatic stabilising device of this kind.

But there is in fact a more fundamental objection to the use of any automatic device of the kind envisaged in the Employment Policy of the White Paper. It is exceedingly difficult to decide to what extent any particular counter-measure to offset inflationary and deflationary developments would be successful in its objective. The economic process in a developed country like the United Kingdom is a complicated system of inter-relationships. An increase in incomes will after a time-lag lead to an increase in the demand for goods and services which in turn after some time-lag is likely to lead to some further increase in incomes paid out to wage-earners and other producers of these goods and services. Increases in expenditure are likely to cause at first some fall in stocks and subsequently both some increase in prices and, after another time-lag, some increase in amounts produced and put on the market for sale. But if prices are rising at a certain rate and have been rising for a certain time, people may be led to speculate upon a continuing rise of prices and they may thus be induced to spend still more on their current purchases of goods; and the rate at which the production of goods is growing may itself influence the amount which is spent in buying new machines and in building up stocks of raw materials and semi-finished goods, in order to keep capital equipment and stocks in balance with a higher rate of output.

Every economist could mention many more dynamic relationships of this kind between movements of prices, costs, profits, wages, tax payments, savings, consumption, investment, output, employment, amounts of money, and rates of interest—to say nothing of the influence of imports, exports, and foreign capital movements. It is into a complicated dynamic system of this kind that the authorities have to introduce their stabilising measures to offset inflationary and deflationary developments of demand in the economic system. Unfortunately much more work must be done on the analysis of such dynamic inter-relationships in the modern economic system before anything can be said with much assurance about the precise effect of any particular stabilising device. Even if it were possible to take some simple criterion (such as the divergence of selling prices above or below some stated ceiling) as the criterion for some stabilising device like variations in national insurance contributions, it would be probable that disinflationary action, and thus the extent of the rise in the level of national insurance contributions, should be intensified not only in accordance with the extent to which the price level is above the ceiling level, but also in accordance both with the speed with which it is still rising and with the extent to which it has been consistently too high over the past. Thus disinflationary action should be strong if prices are too high, have been too high for a long time, and are still rising rapidly. If prices are too high but are already falling rapidly, it may be time to relax the disinflationary pressure in order to make sure that the fall in prices does not overshoot the mark. It may be that when we know much more than we do at present about the nature of reactions within the dynamic economy with which we have to deal, it will be possible to invent an effective automatic formula for stabilisation in which the level of the special stabilisation levy is made to depend automatically on the size, the rate of growth, and the past extent of the divergence between the actual level of prices and the level at which it is desired to stabilise prices.[1] But that time is still far off. For the moment those who are in charge of the operation of such a device must be left with some discretion by trial error to use it in the most effective way to achieve the desired stabilisation.

If this is so, the only way to make the operation of

[1] For a technical discussion of this point see the article by A. W. Philips in the *Economic Journal* for June 1954 entitled 'Stabilisation in a Closed Economy'.

such a device independent of *ad hoc* government decision would be to set up a separate independent statutory body—let us call it the Stabilisation Commission—charged with the task of making variations in the level of the special stabilisation levy at its discretion, but only within the limits laid down by Parliament and only for the purpose of achieving some precisely defined objective, such as the maintenance of total demand for goods and services at the highest possible level compatible with the prevention of some precisely defined price index from rising above a precisely defined ceiling.

The disadvantages of any such arrangement are clear. Budgetary policy, monetary policy, and variations in a special stabilisation levy make up such a closely knit whole that it is inappropriate to have more than one authority with final responsibility for them. Let me give only one example of the problems which might arise if normal budgetary policy were in the hands of the government but special variations in, say, national insurance contributions were in the hands of an independent commission. Suppose that the government were under strong political pressure to reduce taxation at a time of inflationary pressure. If the Chancellor of the Exchequer held the rates of normal taxes at inappropriately low levels, the Stabilisation Commission would have the responsibility of offsetting this by holding the rates of national insurance contributions more or less permanently at abnormally high levels; and this might give an undesirable twist to the distribution of the normal burden of taxation. The only way to avoid this would be to make the Chancellor ultimately responsible for both types of taxation and thus responsible for maintaining a sufficiently strict general monetary and budgetary policy to prevent the need for a permanent use of abnormally high rates for the special stabilisation levies which were intended to be used only for short-term stabilisation purposes.

And yet there is real substance in the argument for removing these month to month stabilisation devices as far from the ordinary political arena as possible. Perhaps a good working arrangement would be to set up a separate Stabilisation Commission to initiate variations in the special stabilisation levies but to put the Commission under the ultimate control of the Chancellor of the Exchequer. The government, by legislation or otherwise, would in this case openly commit itself to the precise objective of maintaining total demand at the highest possible level which was compatible with the prevention of prices from rising above a stated ceiling; two independent bodies, the Bank of England and the Stabilisation Commission, would be given the responsibility for making changes in monetary policy and in the special stabilisation levies for the attainment of this same objective, but they would be subject to final direction by the Chancellor of the Exchequer. To assist the proper co-ordination of the various stabilising devices the Treasury, the Bank of England, and the Stabilisation Commission might be advised by a single expert secretariat; and to ensure a proper public under-standing and appreciation of the stabilisation policy this secretariat might be required to publish an annual report on the stabilisation policies of the Treasury,

Bank of England, and Stabilisation Commission. By such means a full co-ordinated stabilisation policy might be achieved, removed in some degree from the immediate rough and tumble of party politics.

VII

The basic question which I have discussed in this lecture is whether or not the government should put a stop to price inflation once and for all by committing itself so to control the general level of money demand for goods and services that prices are not permitted to rise above a stated ceiling. I have argued that it should be possible to do this, but have pointed out the very real dangers of such a policy, unless wage-fixing methods are suitably reformed. I have illustrated my argument by making a number of positive proposals for the application of such a policy:

First, that the government should accept openly a precise commitment to use its powers of financial policy so as to maintain the highest possible level of demand for goods and services compatible with the prevention of a precisely defined price index from rising above a precisely defined ceiling.

Second, that this price index should be composed of the prices of all home-produced goods and services, exclusive of the prices of imports and the import-content of home production, and exclusive of prices (such as rents) which are subject to important price controls, all prices to be reckoned after the payment of indirect taxes and the receipt of subsidies.

Third, that arrangements should be made for prompt and frequent variations in some suitable widespread levy on personal incomes as an additional means of controlling demand.

Fourth, that a Stabilisation Commission, subject to the ultimate control of the Chancellor of the Exchequer, should be set up to determine and operate these variations in the special stabilisation levies.

Fifth, that the Treasury, the Bank of England, and the Stabilisation Commission should share a common technical secretariat to give advice on stabilisation policies, and that this secretariat should publish an annual report on the stabilisation policies which had been adopted.

Sixth, that some body like the Council on Prices, Productivity and Incomes, should at regular intervals publish an estimate of the average rates of rise in money wage earnings per head which it considered would be compatible with the preservation of full employment in these conditions of stable selling prices.

Seventh, that arbitral bodies should be set up to which employers, workers, or the government could refer for a judgement whether the workers involved in any particular wage negotiation should obtain a rise in wage earnings appreciably above or below the average in order, over the next few years, to avoid a serious local shortage or redundancy of labour.

Eighth, that more extensive provision should be made to ease the retraining, removal, and rehousing of workers who become redundant in their existing jobs.

Ninth, that restrictive practices in the labour market should not be exempt from public scrutiny and control.

Tenth, that if financial policies were concentrated on domestic stability in this way, variations in the rate of exchange between the pound and other currencies could and should be made much more freely as a means of preserving equilibrium in the balance of payments.

I have put forward these proposals in a very positive tone of voice. But whether or not the government should actually take the plunge depends both upon questions of fact such as how much unemployment would in fact be necessary in any given circumstances to avoid a cost inflation and also upon value judgements such as how much unemployment it would be worth risking in order to achieve price stability. I have not tried in this lecture to answer either of these questions; I have tried only to elucidate some of the processes at work. The detailed proposals which I have put forward so brashly are intended mainly as illustrations of these processes. I rather think that I myself believe in them; but my main purpose has been to use them as illustrations of the basic issues.

VIII

One final word. My lecture has been about the control of inflation, because that is the problem with which we have become so familiar in recent years. I do not myself believe much in forecasting economic events. But it is at least possible that in the not too far distant future inflationary pressures may give place for a time to deflationary forces. A more serious American recession than anything which we have experienced since the end of the Second World War is always a possibility. In such an event we should have to put the engines of financial policy rapidly and massively into reverse. One of the main virtues which I would claim for proposals of the type which I have outlined today is that they are equally well designed to stimulate expenditure and to keep selling prices up in a period of deflationary pressure as they are to prevent price rises in an otherwise inflationary situation; and it is even more important to be in a position to offset any future deflation than to stop the present inflation.

©

CAMBRIDGE UNIVERSITY PRESS

1958

This inaugural lecture, delivered in Cambridge on 4 March 1958 by J. E. Meade, C.B., F.B.A., M.A., Professor of Political Economy in the University of Cambridge, was published in 1958 by the Syndics of the Cambridge University Press and printed in Great Britain at the University Press, Cambridge (Brooke Crutchley, University Printer).